creative albums

by Donna Downey

Founding Editor | Stacy Julian

Editor-in-Chief | Lin Sorenson

Editors | Valerie Pingree, Elisha Snow

Editorial Assistant | Carolyn Jolley

Copy Editor | Mark Zoellner

Art Director | Don Lambson

Graphic Designer | Cathy Zielske

Photography | John Luke

Vice President, Group Publisher | David O'Neil

SVP, Group Publishing Director | Scott Wagner

VP, Group CFO | Henry Donahue

For information on carrying *Simple Scrapbooks* products in your retail
store, please call (800) 815-3583. For information on ordering *Simple
Scrapbooks* magazine, call toll-free (866) 334-8149. *Simple Scrapbooks*
is located at 14850 Pony Express Road, Bluffdale, Utah, 84065. Phone:
(801) 984-2070. Home page: *www.simplescrapbooksmag.com*

Printed in Korea
ISBN 1 929180 78 0

creative albums

a guide to the projects

8   supplies

10   adhesive

12   tools

15   techniques

118   resources

THE DOWNEY FAMILY

2003 2003 2003 2003 2003

a year
in
review

CREATE

A self-proclaimed "paper product junkie," Donna Downey notes that scrapbooking is the ideal extension of her paper and photography addiction. As a contributing editor for *Simple Scrapbooks* magazine, she plays with the latest and greatest products, yet manages to keep the projects—and the process—simple and do-able.

Donna travels and teaches at scrapbook events across the country, inspiring students to think outside of the traditional scrapbook box, while still preserving their memories in a meaningful way.

A former elementary school teacher, Donna is a stay-at-home mom to her three children, McKenna, Payton and Cole. Originally from the Jersey shore, she now lives in North Carolina and teaches at her local scrapbook store. She tries to steal away as much quiet time as she can to scrapbook—which usually means she kicks it into gear at 1 a.m.

PLAY

LIVE

CAROLYN VAUGHN PHOTOGRAPHY

119

yes, it's a scrapbook!

LOOK FOR MORE BOOKS BY DONNA DOWNEY

photo decor

Twenty-five amazing ways to display
memories and photos on the table or on the
wall. Step-by-step instructions and photos.

$14.95. 120 pages.

decorative journals

Twenty-five unique ideas for saving the
story of special moments and everyday life.
Step-by-step instructions and photos.

$14.95. 120 pages.

To order, call toll-free (866) 334-8149, visit your scrapbook store,
or shop online at **simplescrapbooksmag.com/shop**

creative albums

a guide to the projects

18   2003 year in review | ALTERED CD ALBUM

22   best friends forever | ACCORDION POCKET ALBUM

26   my little book of four-letter words | TAG ALBUM

30   coley | SLIDE MOUNT ACCORDION ALBUM

34   art | BOUND PAINT CHIP ALBUM

38   understanding 3 | CARDBOARD ALBUM

42   simply payton | CD TIN ALBUM

46   grandma stephan | CIGAR BOX ALBUM

50   a room with a view | PLEXIGLAS ALBUM

54   signs of home | SPIRAL-BOUND ALBUM

58   before i was a mom | GATED ALBUM

62   my travels | CANVAS MAT BOARD ALBUM

66   what do you do all day? | POST-BOUND ALBUM

8   supplies

10   adhesive

12   tools

15   techniques

118   resources

70   circle of friends | BLUE JEAN CHIPBOARD ALBUM

74   a true friend | COIN ENVELOPE ALBUM

78   family | ENVELOPE ACCORDION ALBUM

82   favorite family photos 2004 | SHUTTERFLY PHOTO ALBUM

86   soccer 2004 | FLIP-FLOP ACCORDION ALBUM

90   a lifetime of memories | ROLODEX ALBUM

94   through the years | 4" X 6" PHOTO ALBUM

98   family recipes | BINDER BOARD ALBUM

102   confessions of a shopaholic | SHOPPING BAG ALBUM

106   love | MINI-BOX ACCORDION ALBUM

110   cole | FLOPPY DISK ALBUM

114   you-nique | CLIPBOARD ALBUM

dedication

To my husband, Bill: you've not only let me be my own person, but you've supported me through every endeavor I've undertaken. You've given me a security and a sense of self I'd never known before…I love you.

To my children, McKenna, Payton, and Cole: you are my inspiration, my devotion and my heart.

To my best friend, Karen: after 20 years you're still keeping me grounded and laughing. You're an amazing person, and I'm so lucky to know you.

To all my girlfriends, especially Debbie, Vicky, and Barb: even though you've never scrapbooked (nor wanted to) a day in your life, you never once hesitated when asked to complete pages for my scrapbook.

To all my friends at Scrapbooks 'N More: you challenge and inspire me. Thanks for your willingness to play outside of the box.

this is fun stuff

I'VE ALWAYS BELIEVED THAT ANYTHING THAT brings together treasured photographs and the stories behind them should fall under the umbrella of scrapbooking. It doesn't matter whether you're "crafty" or not, surrounding yourself with the evidence of your life and memories preserved is an uplifting and positive thing.

Creating a traditional scrapbook is not enticing to everyone. Frankly, it takes a good chunk of time to assemble an album full of pages. This is why we at *Simple Scrapbooks* magazine are so thrilled to bring you the first of Donna's books. She looks at everyday things differently than most of us. She'll open your eyes to dozens of cool possibilities and show you that when it comes to celebrating life with pictures and written words, there are endless options. Some of the projects in this book can be whipped up in an afternoon; some may take a day or two. With the step-by-step instructions here, all are extremely do-able.

After seeing Donna's projects firsthand, I was completely and totally energized, rendered sleepless for several nights, and moved to order six Rolodex files and 18 clipboards online. Trust me, this is fun stuff.

STACY JULIAN, FOUNDING EDITOR

YOU WILL NEVER LOOK AT A CIGAR

BOX THE SAME WAY AGAIN

think outside the cigar box!

AS A CHILD I CREATED AN ENTIRE PURSE
and its contents from a stack of blank, mustard-yellow
8½" x 11" paper. Wallet, lipstick, money and checkbook
were all contained in my paper purse and held together
by staples. It should have been clear then that I was either
going to be a very poor fashion designer or a scrapbooker.

My creativity has been running amok since then, and
shows no signs of letting up. When I cruise the aisles
of any store, I can't stop my brain from thinking, "Hey,
I could make a scrapbook from that." Paper bags are
never just something to haul groceries; they're scrapbooks to showcase my shopping addiction. Cigar boxes
are more than musty containers to hold stogies; they're
scrapbooks chronicling the life of my husband's grandmother. Sure, I still scrapbook pages in traditional albums,
but now I try to look at my pictures with a critical eye
when developing non-traditional concept albums.

People always ask me, "How did you think of that?"
I don't know the answer. I guess I'm looking for the
scrapbook in everything. Whenever I find something I
would like to make into an album, I always consider
how the material can be bound and turned into pages
before I think about photos. Next comes the memory,

a moment, an event, or possibly just a really cool series
of pictures that depict ordinary life. I'm inspired by *all*
products—not just traditional scrapbooking supplies.
And I'm excited by the strangest things—like old CDs.
It drives my family crazy.

Consider this book your chance to cut loose. Have fun,
be creative, go wild. Drive *your* family crazy. Change,
alter, or modify these projects to suit your whims. But
above all, these scrapbooks are meant to be displayed
and handled often. They invite people to touch and
look through them, and that's the best part. These
aren't museum displays—they should be dog-eared,
threadbare, banged up, and well-worn after six months.
If they're not, you should be inviting more people over
for a visit.

Enjoy this first installment of *Yes, It's a Scrapbook!* You'll
never look at a cigar box the same way again.

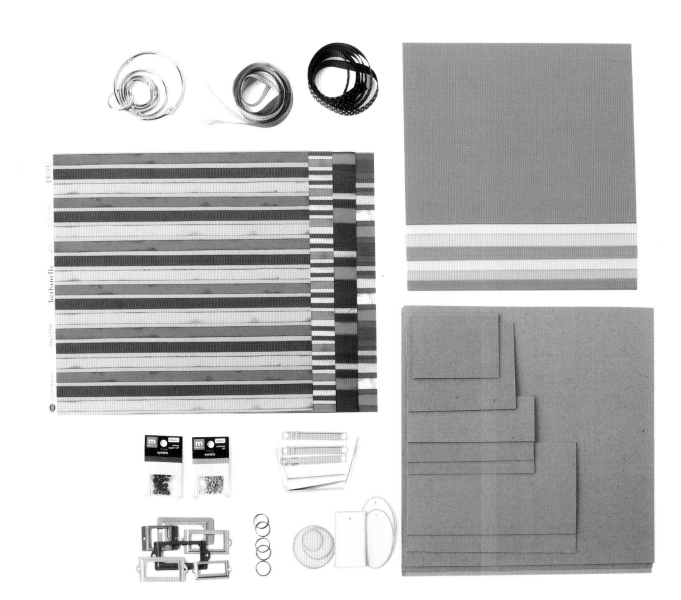

supplies

Here are a handful of basic items I used to make the albums in this book. Most of these supplies can be found at craft, scrapbook, or office supply stores. Each project lists the generic supplies under the "Supplies" section and the specific manufacturer or source under the "Materials" section. If you find something that works better than what I've listed, then by all means experiment and have fun. There's no such thing as mistakes—just be creative. *Note: Some items listed in the "Supplies" section are not repeated in the "Materials" section.*

Binder rings
Steel rings that pull open, traditionally used to hold papers together.

Bookplates
Small metal frames, available in a variety of shapes, styles and finishes.

Brads
Fasteners with metal prongs that spread behind paper to hold the brad in place.

Cardstock
Heavyweight, preferably acid-free paper for paper crafting.

Chipboard
Thin, durable cardboard used to create album covers and project pages. Check with your local scrapbook stores. Most wholesale packs of paper use chipboard to prevent bending during shipping, and stores may be discarding it without realizing its potential. Visit *dickblick.com* or *vanguardcrafts.com* for more information.

Eyelets
Small fasteners inserted into punched holes. Eyelets add a finished look once set in place. Available in many shapes, sizes, and colors.

Jump rings
Split metal rings used to dangle embellishments.

Patterned paper
Offered in an assortment of styles and colors, patterned paper can set the tone for an entire project. To make your patterned paper choices easier, try choosing from product lines that offer coordinated sets.

Prong fasteners
Two-piece metal clips that bind sheets of paper together, and can be found at most office supply stores.

Ribbon
Available in craft, fabric, and scrapbook stores, ribbon is an easy way to add color and texture to a project.

Tags
Metal-rimmed tags are available in a variety of shapes, sizes, styles, and colors, while shipping tags—usually rectangular—also work well.

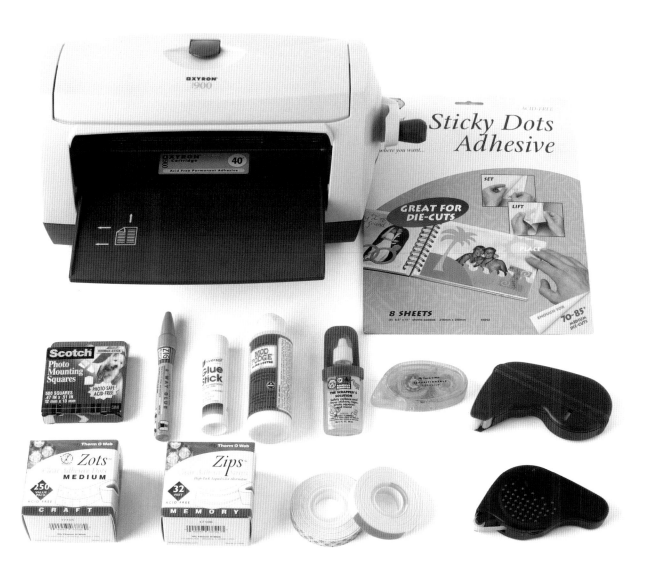

adhesive

All adhesives are not created equal. But that doesn't mean you can't make substitutions. Each project in this book lists a preferred adhesive, but if you have something on hand that works just as well or you like better, then that's fine, too. Listed below are some of the most common adhesives.

CLEAR ADHESIVE DOTS AND STRIPS

Dots
Small circles of double-sided adhesive. Available in a variety of sizes and thicknesses. Perfect for adhering small embellishments, metal and leather, as well as unusally-shaped or heavy objects.

Strips
Thin strips of double-sided adhesive. Perfect for adhering long thin objects, such as ribbon, to a project. A good alternative to hot glue.

DOUBLE-SIDED TAPES

Tape runners (refillable)
Clear, double-sided, acid-free adhesive. Available in permanent and repositionable types.

Tab dispensers (refillable)
Applies acid-free squares of double-sided tabs.

Dot dispensers
Applies double-sided, acid-free dot adhesive. Available in permanent and repositionable types.

Photo tabs
Double-sided, acid-free adhesive squares.

Tape
Sold by the roll and can be cut to desired length.

Pop-up dots and foam tape
Three-dimensional, double-sided adhesive.

FULL-SURFACE ADHESIVE

Xyron machine
Functions as a "sticker maker," covering the entire surface of paper with adhesive.

Decoupage adhesive
Commonly referred to as Mod Podge, this water-based sealer, glue and finish is used best when covering a large project area with paper. Available in glossy, matte, and acid-free varieties.

Dot adhesive sheets
Tiny adhesive dots that transfer from sheets of release paper by pressing items, such as die cuts, to the dots. The dots attach only where needed.

Glue stick
Inexpensive alternative for applying adhesive to a large surface area, but best suited for paper-to-paper applications.

REMOVERS

Adhesive eraser
Quickly rubs away any excess adhesive.

Adhesive remover
Commonly referred to as Un-du, this liquid adhesive remover easily lifts stickers, labels, and all kinds of adhesive from surfaces without harm. Liquid quickly evaporates, and items are restored to their original tackiness. Remover will not harm photos.

tools

These projects require few tools. But listed below are the ones that will certainly come in handy as you complete the projects in this book.

Bone folder
Once made from bone, these plastic folders are used to score paper or cardstock and create professional-looking projects. To use, create a crease with the tip of the bone folder. Then, fold the paper on the crease and use the flat side of the folder to smooth out the fold completely.

Brayer
A roller that helps remove bubbles under paper to prevent paper from lifting in the future. For example, after applying a layer of decoupage adhesive and paper to a project, roll the brayer over the surface to smooth away any trapped air bubbles.

Computer
By no means a necessary tool, a computer with a word processing program (such as Microsoft Word) can help you generate text for journaling, or print on cardstock or embellishments. Handwritten text and journaling works just as well.

Cutting template
An acrylic template-based cutting system, such as the Coluzzle, requires the use of a swivel knife and foam cutting mat.

Labeler
A hand-held, turn-and-click label strip embosser.

Eyelet-setting tools
Eyelet-setting tools consist of four parts:

> Mat or board—protects work surface from damage when using tools.
>
> Small craft hammer—applies force to eyelet tools.
>
> Anywhere hole punch—punches an eyelet-sized hole in your paper or project.
>
> Eyelet setter—finishes and secures eyelet.

Craft hand drill
Hand-powered craft drill, especially useful when binding projects and albums. *Note: Be sure to use a safe drilling surface. Do not apply too much pressure—all you need is light pressure and a fast drilling hand.*

tools

Craft knife
A pen-like cutting blade used to trim paper in tight or unusually-shaped areas (also known as an X-acto knife).

Foam brushes
Inexpensive and disposable craft brushes are great for applying paint and liquid adhesives to projects.

Paper trimmer
A straight-line paper cutter, sized to accommodate paper up to 12" wide, with an extending ruler arm for measuring. Interchangeable scoring blades for paper trimmers mark an impression in paper, making it easier to fold.

Paper piercer
A sharp-pointed tool used to poke guide holes in paper. You can substitute a sewing needle or push pin.

Punch pad
A foam mat used to absorb the point of pierced applications. You can substitute a foam mouse pad.

Sanding block
Foam core sanding blocks provide more surface area to grip while sanding. However, any medium to fine grade sandpaper will do.

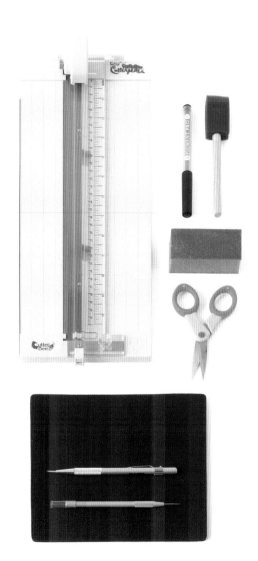

techniques

The projects in this book use only a handful of techniques, all of them relatively simple. Refer to this quick guide when you need help.

WRAPPING CHIPBOARD

ASSEMBLING ACCORDION PAGES

SANDING

Wrapping Chipboard Covers

1. Trim paper, leaving 1" allowance on all edges.

2. Apply adhesive to back side of paper.

3. Center chipboard over back side of paper and adhere.

4. Fold over corners, then wrap excess paper around chipboard. *Note: Folding the corners first will create a nice seam. You can use the flat side of a bone folder to secure the folds.*

Assembling Accordion Pages

1. Cut 12" x 12" cardstock into strips. The width of the strips will depend on how tall you want your album—for example, 12" x 2", 12" x 4", or 12" x 6". The number of strips will determine how long you want your album.

2. Accordion-fold each strip, using a bone folder (see "Bone folder" on p. 13). The width of each fold will determine the width of the finished album. For example, fold every 2", 3", or 4".

3. Adhere the last panel of one strip under the first panel of the next strip.

Sanding

1. To create an aged, weathered look, rough up the edges of your paper or project with a sanding block.

2. To create a finished edge, sand the edges of paper that has been adhered to a project instead of cutting it to fit.

techniques

Setting Eyelets

(See "Eyelet-setting tools" on p. 13)

1. Place pointed end of anywhere hole punch on spot where you want eyelet. Hit 2–3 times firmly with hammer to create hole.

2. Lay eyelet upside down; place hole over eyelet.

3. Place setter into eyelet, and hammer firmly to set eyelet in place. *Note: The force of the hammer will cause the eyelet back to "flower" and secure to the page.*

4. Remove setter, and hammer eyelet once or twice to flatten completely. Turn over.

Inking

To achieve a weathered, vintage look, gently rub a stamp pad across the edges of your pages or project.

Chalking

For a more dramatic aged look, ink your cardstock, then immediately use a cotton ball to rub a small amount of grey chalk over your ink. As it is drying, the ink will absorb the chalk.

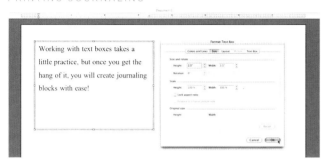

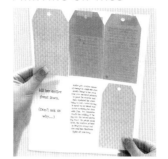

Printing Journaling

There are two ways to print journaling in Microsoft Word. (For both ways, make sure you measure the finished size of the journaling area.)

1. Set margins
   a. Open a new Word document.
   b. Make sure there is a visible ruler running across the top of your document. If not, click View > Ruler.
   c. To set margins, click File > Page Setup. Based on the finished size of your journaling, type in margin sizes for the top, bottom, left, and right. Click OK.
   d. The new margins will be represented by highlighted sections on the page rulers.

2. Create text box
   a. Follow Steps a and b above.
   b. Click Insert > Text Box. Click and drag mouse to draw text box.
   c. Click Format > Text Box > Size. Set the size of the text box the same as the finished size of your journaling area. Click OK. *Note: To remove box lines, click Format > Text Box > Colors and Lines. Select "No Fill" for Fill/Color. Select "No Line" for Line/Color.*
   d. Type journaling and print.

Printing Text on Tags

1. Type and print test page on computer paper.
2. Hold test page up to light and position tag behind text to ensure text will fit on tag.
3. Adhere tag over text using repositionable adhesive.
4. Reload test page and print text on tag. *Note: It's easier to print on tags (especially metal-rimmed tags) using a top-loading printer.* Remove tag and rub off adhesive.

Printing Reverse Text

1. Follow Steps a-d under "Create text box."
2. Change the background color by clicking Format > Text Box > Colors and Lines. Select the color you want under the "Fill" section.
3. Change the font color to white by clicking Format > Font > Font Color. If needed, center text in text box by clicking Format > Paragraph > Alignment > Center.
4. Print out on white paper or cardstock. Note: For crisper text, print on photo paper.

THE DOWNEY FAMILY

2003 2003 2003 2003 2003

a year
in
review

2003 year in review

This album was the original inspiration for the *Yes, It's a Scrapbook!* series, and proves that when it comes to compiling, arranging, and displaying bound memories, it's good to think outside the box. It's a great way to use those old CDs you don't listen to anymore—and unless someone peels back the paper, no one ever has to know you were once the world's biggest Kenny Loggins fan.

| labeler | **ADHESIVE** |
| scissors | • Xyron machine |

- labeler
- scissors

MATERIALS

patterned paper (Chatterbox) • metal-rimmed tags (Avery Dennison) • rub-ons (Chartpak) • stickers (Creative Imaginations, Li'l Davis Designs, EK Success) • word plaque (Li'l Davis Designs) • metal letters, word, bookplate (Making Memories) • stamp pad (Ranger Industries) • Coluzzle nested circle template, swivel knife, mat (Provo Craft) • labeler (Dymo) • hand drill (Fiskars)

STEP SEVEN

Drill second hole using smallest drill bit. *Note: For a random effect, drill the small hole in a different spot on each CD so that the tags will extend from all sides of your final album.* Thread jump rings with tags through small holes in CDs.

STEP EIGHT

Embellish CDs using rub-ons; embellish small tags using stickers.

STEP NINE

Attach all CDs to large binder ring.

Helpful Tip

When using the Coluzzle template, the large circle template—the sixth circle from the center—is the exact size for the CDs. If you do not have the large template, you can trace a CD and cut by hand or use a smaller circle for your pages.

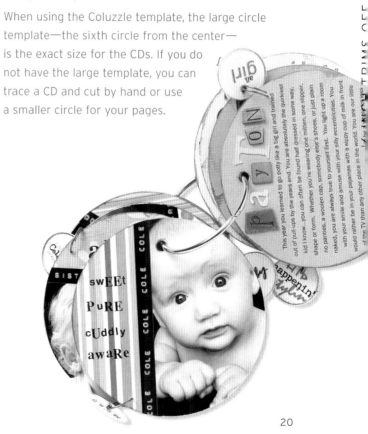

SUPPLIES

- eight compact discs
- eight 6" x 6" pieces of coordinated patterned paper
- eight 6" x 6" pieces of cardstock
- seven 4" x 6" photos
- stamp pad
- seven metal-rimmed tags with jump rings and 2½" binder ring
- rub-on letters
- stickers, cut to small round tag size

TOOLS

- large circle template
- swivel knife and mat
- hand drill with largest and smallest drill bits

altered cd album step-by-step

STEP ONE

Use circle template or trace CD to cut eight circles, one from each piece of patterned paper.

STEP TWO

Ink edges of patterned paper (see "Inking" on p. 16) and adhere pieces to one side of each CD. *Note: Use a full-surface adhesive to prevent the edges of your papers and photos from lifting.*

STEP THREE

Use template or CD to round off each photo. *Note: The straight edge of the photo should fit about halfway to three quarters across the CD.* Adhere photos to CD, over patterned paper.

STEP FOUR

Use labeler to create word strips. Adhere word strips along straight edge of photos.

STEP FIVE

Print or write text on cardstock pieces and trim to circles using template or CD. Ink edges and adhere to back of CDs. *Note: If you choose to print your text, create a text box no larger than 3" x 4" (see "Printing Journaling" on p. 17).*

STEP SIX

Using largest drill bit, drill hole at top of each CD for binder ring (see "Craft hand drill" on p. 13).

best friends forever

I've known my best friend Karen for almost 20 years, and that's a lot of late-night chats and secrets. A friendship like ours deserves a special album, so I created this one, complete with little tags describing our years together (and the trouble we caused). All you need is one piece of 12" x 12" cardstock to create the accordion, and, of course, a dear friend to share it.

MATERIALS

patterned paper, pre-printed quotes (KI Memories) · tags (DMD, Inc.) · frame, photo turn (7gypsies) · bookplate (Li'l Davis Designs) · eyelets, brad (Making Memories) · ribbons (May Arts, Textured Trios, The Weathered Door)

STEP EIGHT
Fold top outside corners of first and last panels toward inside creases, and secure using eyelets (see "Setting Eyelets" on p. 16).

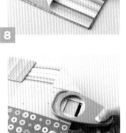

STEP NINE
Use square punch to create windows in second and third panels.

STEP TEN
Embellish four tags, using ribbon, photos, patterned paper, and quotes.

STEP ELEVEN
Unfold cardstock. Place tags within open folds of four panels; refold cardstock in half.

STEP TWELVE
Embellish album using additional quotes. Adhere frame with dots. Attach photo turn with brad. Place quotes behind frame and photo turn.

STEP THIRTEEN
Print album title. Mount title and bookplate on cover.

accordion pocket album step-by-step

STEP ONE

Fold cardstock in half, using bone folder (see "Bone folder" on p. 13). Unfold. Accordion-fold lengthwise every 3". Refold cardstock in half.

STEP TWO

To create front and back covers, adhere 5" x 8" patterned paper pieces to chipboard, using Xyron machine (see "Wrapping Chipboard Covers" on p. 15). Sand edges.

STEP THREE

Before assembling album, make sure the long, folded edge of accordion-folded cardstock is at the bottom. Attach cover to front flap, making sure it opens to the left.

STEP FOUR

Before adhering back cover, adhere ribbon to back of album. Wrap around album and tie in front.

STEP FIVE

Turn album over and attach back cover over ribbon, securing ribbon in place. *Note: Make sure the cover opens to the right.*

STEP SIX

Using photo tabs, adhere four pieces of 3" x 6" patterned paper to four inside panels.

STEP SEVEN

Adhere two remaining 3" x 6" patterned paper pieces to the back of first and last panels.

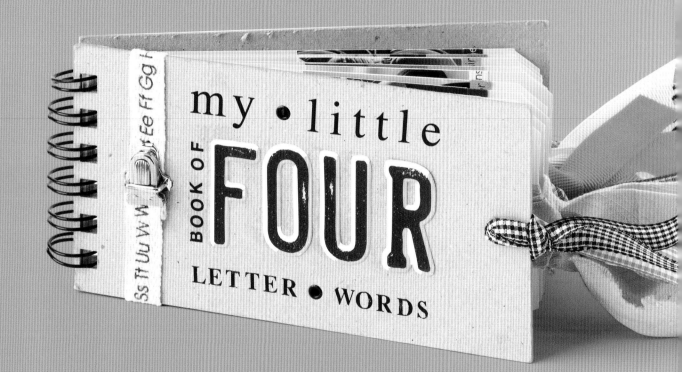

my little book of four-letter words

This little tag book is filled with some of my favorite *clean* four-letter words. It's a scrapbook just for me, and it sits in plain view on my desk. It's the first thing people reach for when they walk into my workspace, and the last thing they put down before they leave. Sure, it's starting to show some signs of wear, but that's the best compliment of all.

MATERIALS

tag book, printed twill ribbon, buckle fastener (7gypsies) • ribbon
(Offray, Textured Trios) • rub-ons (Chartpak) • letter stickers (Sticker
Studio) • eyelets (Making Memories) • pen (Sakura)

Helpful Tip

Make your own tag book, or buy a pre-made one from
companies such as 7gypsies, K&Company, or Rusty Pickle.

tag album step-by-step

STEP ONE
Trim photos to fit one tag, approximately 2¼" x 3⅛". Adhere photos to the right of each page.

STEP TWO
Use letter stickers to create four-letter words. Place vertically to the left of each photo.

STEP THREE
Print or handwrite two cardstock word strips for each page. Cut and adhere strip next to photo. Cut and adhere strip on back next to spiral binding.

STEP FOUR
Set eyelets through word strip on back, making sure the finished side of the eyelet shows on the front of the tag.

STEP FIVE
Handwrite journaling on the back of each tag. Use chalk to highlight important words.

STEP SIX
Tie ribbon through hole of each tag.

STEP SEVEN
Embellish cover using letter stickers, rub-ons, printed twill ribbon, eyelets, and buckle fastener.

coley

Our Grandma Cookie works at the deli counter at the local supermarket and is all the talk every time she pulls one of these grandchildren-filled mini albums from her purse. These scrapbooks fit in the palm of her hand, so she can whip one out sometime between dispensing the Gouda and smoked turkey, to show off these sweet faces. It's the perfect brag book.

Whether it's Cole. Coley, Coler, Cola, Cole-Baby or Little Man you come smiling and crawling no matter what. Perhaps the happiest and sweetest little boy I have ever seen, it is hard not to squeeze and kiss you every moment of the day. Your expressions are priceless and those meaty little thighs just delicious to nibble on. As you continue to grow and change, it is great to see you develop such a playful personality.

journaled 9.04

ADHESIVE
- **double-sided tape**

MATERIALS

slide mounts (Design Originals) • rub-ons, definition stickers, stencil letter (Making Memories) • ribbon (May Arts, Textured Trios)

STEP SEVEN

Trim photos and any journaling to 3¼" squares. Adhere and embellish with rub-ons, ribbon, charm, stencil letter, and stickers.

slide mount accordion album step-by-step

STEP ONE

Score each cardstock strip every 3½". Accordion-fold.

STEP TWO

Adhere accordion strips together by overlapping ends (see "Assembling Accordion Pages" on p. 15).

STEP THREE

Trim any extra panels so that the two ends face up.

STEP FOUR

Slip photos into slide mounts, and adhere so that the photo is facing out the window.

STEP FIVE

Adhere slide mount to the front of your accordion strip.

STEP SIX

Before adhering back cover, adhere ribbon to back of accordion strip—then wrap around album. Tie in front. Adhere back slide mount to accordion strip, securing ribbon in place.

art

Seems like someone in my house is always painting, drawing, scribbling, or crafting something. The place buzzes with artistic energy, and I always feel compelled to capture it on film. With stacks of multicolor photos to show for my neurosis, I have a creative solution for the photo overload—use ordinary paint chips from your local hardware store to create a scrapbook.

MATERIALS

patterned paper (Paper House Productions) • paint chips (Glidden) • ribbon (Paper House Productions, Textured Trios, May Arts) • chipboard, puzzle, wooden letters (Li'l Davis Designs) • rubber stamps (All Night Media, Inkadinkado) • rub-ons (Creative Imaginations) • woven label (me & my BIG ideas) • spiral clip, brad (Making Memories) • word charm (*stampersanonymous.com*) • tile letter (Junkitz) • labeler (Dymo) • adhesive remover (Un-du)

album where the paint chip ends extend past the template. Do not bind on the folds. Once bound, remove templates from paint chip pages, using adhesive remover.

STEP SIX
Trim photos to 2½" x 3½". Adhere to paint strips. Embellish using ribbon, stickers, charms, and journaling.

STEP SEVEN
Tie ribbons to spine.

bound paint chip album step-by-step

STEP ONE

Wrap chipboard pieces, using 7" x 12" pieces of patterned paper (see "Wrapping Chipboard Covers" on p. 15).

STEP TWO

Adhere 4¾" x 9¾" pieces of cardstock to inside of each cover to conceal unfinished sides.

STEP THREE

To create the pages, fold each paint chip in half lengthwise with a bone folder. (See "Bone folder" on p. 13).

STEP FOUR

Starting from the bottom, layer six of the paint chips on 3" x 10" piece of cardstock. *Note: The cardstock is a template and will ensure the album is bound correctly.* Arrange chips about 1¼" apart, folded edge flush with the template edge. Leave ¼" space at the top and bottom of the template. Adhere with photo tabs. Layer and adhere six more paint strips on the second template.

STEP FIVE

Take covers and paint strips (on templates) to local office supply or copy store to have the album professionally wire-bound. *Note: Bind the*

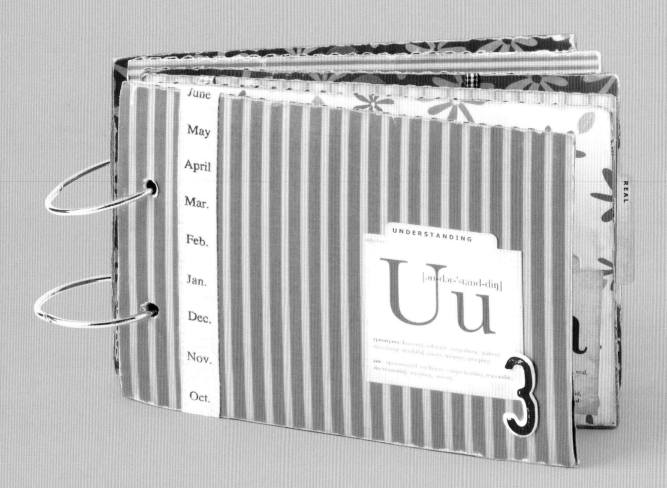

understanding 3

CARDBOARD ALBUM

One man's trash is certainly a scrapper's treasure. Pull that cardboard box from your recycling bin, 'cause it's a scrapbook. Layered with texture and sentiment, this album is the perfect complement to my daughter McKenna's rough-and-tumble tomboy exterior and her tender, sensitive spirit. Plus, the texture of the cardboard is just plain cool.

MATERIALS

printed twill, ribbon (7gypsies) • synonym tabs, rub-on date (Autumn Leaves) • number sticker (Sticker Studio) • ribbon (Offray) • Times New Roman font • stamp pad (Ranger Industries)

STEP SEVEN

Add photos and inked synonym tabs to the front of each page. Tie ribbons around a few pages.

STEP EIGHT

Embellish cover using twill ribbon, inked synonym tab, and number sticker.

cardboard album step-by-step

STEP ONE

Peel away the top layer of the large and small cardboard pages to reveal the corrugation.

STEP TWO

Adhere 6" x 9" pieces of patterned paper to the smooth (uncorrugated) sides of the larger cardboard pages.

STEP THREE

For the smaller pages, print or write journaling on cardstock and adhere to the smooth sides. Ink edges (see "Inking" on p. 16).

STEP FOUR

Print or write journaling on tags and adhere to the corrugated backs of the larger pages (see "Printing Text on Tags" on p. 17).

STEP FIVE

For each large page, punch two holes approx. ¾" from the left side of the page, and 1¾" from the top and bottom. For each small page, punch two holes approx. ¾" from the left side of the page, and 1½" from the top and bottom. *Note: Make sure that the journaling is on the back of all the pages.*

STEP SIX

Place pages on binder rings, alternating large and small pages.

simply payton

Dangling from a hook next to my daughter's bed, this album has affectionately become known as Payton's "shiny round me book." Every night it's her book of choice before bed, and even though at three she can't read a word of it, she flips through it again and again, asking me to read it to her. For Payton, it's the best bedtime story in the world.

- eyelet-setting tools
- paper trimmer
- 3" circle punch

ADHESIVE
- photo tabs

MATERIALS

CD tin (Scrapbooks 'N More) • patterned paper, pre-printed transparency (Creative Imaginations) • ribbon (Offray) • metal-rimmed tag, eyelets, jump ring (Making Memories) • Univers Light Ultra Condensed font • Coluzzle nested circle template, swivel knife, mat (Provo Craft) • hand drill (Fiskars)

STEP SIX

Adhere reinforcement labels around the drilled holes on both the front and back of each page.

STEP SEVEN

Trace and cut four circles from patterned paper. Cut circles in half and adhere half circle to one-half of each page.

STEP EIGHT

Punch a photo for each page, using jumbo circle punch. Adhere photo to page.

STEP NINE

Print or write title on the vellum tag (see "Printing Text on Tags" on p. 17). Add jump ring.

STEP TEN

Thread ribbon through tin, pages, transparency and jump ring. Tie in bow.

Helpful Tip

The Coluzzle nested circle template has eight circles to choose from. The sixth circle from the center happens to be the exact size of a CD. If you don't have this template-based cutting system, you can always trace a CD and cut by hand.

cd tin album step-by-step

STEP ONE

Cut each sheet of 12" x 12" cardstock into four 6" squares. Create appropriate-sized text boxes. Print or write text and journaling on both sides of squares (see "Printing Journaling" on p. 17). Use circle template (see "Cutting template" on p. 13) or trace CD to cut four circles from each sheet. *Note: You will have a total of eight circles.*

STEP TWO

Cut circle from printed transparency.

STEP THREE

Drill holes through the closed CD tin. *Note: You'll need to secure the tin with a clamp, or have someone hold the tin in place while you drill.*

STEP FOUR

Set an eyelet in both the top and bottom of the tin, making sure to set the finished side of the eyelet on the outside of the tin.

STEP FIVE

Use the tin lid to mark where to drill holes on circle pages, including the transparency. Mark first page and drill through all nine pages at once.

43

grandma stephan

I had covered a cigar box with decorative paper and it sat on my desk for about a month. I would walk past it and say, "That really looks pretty," and keep on walking. About this time I was interviewing my husband's grandmother about her life, knowing that her story would make a great keepsake one day. I typed it all up on my computer and tucked it away in a cyber file. Finally one day, it made sense: the two things, the cigar box and the interview, just had to go together.

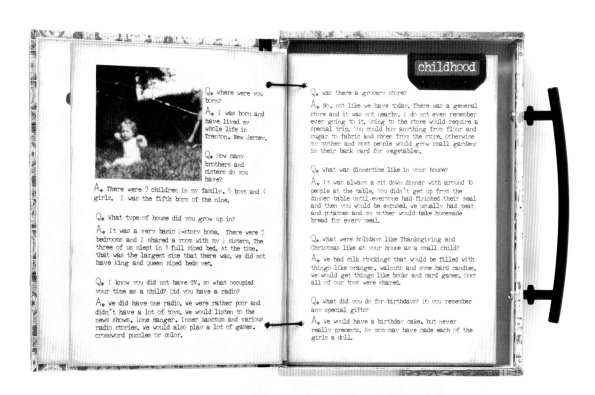

STEP FIVE

With smaller drill bit, drill two holes each through box lid and base (approx. $\frac{3}{4}$" from the spine and $1\frac{3}{8}$" from each side).

STEP SIX

Print album title on cardstock. Trim cardstock $\frac{1}{4}$" smaller than inside box lid on all sides. Ink edges and adhere to inside lid. Use labeler to create strip of text. Place along bottom edge of cardstock where lid meets base.

STEP SEVEN

To create album pages, print text on cardstock, leaving room for photos. Trim cardstock to 6" x 8$\frac{1}{2}$". Ink edges and adhere photos.

STEP EIGHT

Adhere cardstock pages, one each to the front and back of chipboard pieces.

STEP NINE

Using small bit, drill holes through pages (approx. $\frac{1}{2}$" from side and 1" from top and bottom (see photo). Thread elastic through the bottom of the box, up through the pages, and through the top of the box.

Helpful Tip

If you don't have a cigar box, you can use a stationery or gift box.

SUPPLIES

- 9½" x 7" cigar box
- three 12" x 12" pieces of patterned paper
- five 6" x 8½" pieces of chipboard
- 11 8½" x 11" pieces of cardstock
- two 2" elastic cords with metal stops
- drawer pull
- stamp pad

TOOLS

- foam brush
- paper towels
- brayer
- hand drill with large and second smallest drill bits

cigar box album step-by-step

STEP ONE

Trim patterned paper to fit each of the four small sides and the back of the box. *Note: You may want to cut your paper slightly larger than your surface areas, then use a sanding block to sand away the over-hanging edges. This will also create a nice aged look.* Brush a moderate coat of decoupage adhesive on box sides and adhere paper. Firmly press in place and smooth with paper towel, making sure to wipe away any excess adhesive. Use brayer to roll over surface and smooth away any trapped air bubbles.

STEP TWO

Trim patterned paper to fit the top of the box. Adhere using decoupage adhesive. Use a craft knife to cut the paper so the lid can open.

STEP THREE

Let dry in the open position. Gently sand the edges to remove any excess glue.

STEP FOUR

Drill two holes in the box front with a large bit, and install drawer pull. *Note: Drawer pulls usually come with coordinating screws. Depending on the thickness of your box, you may need to purchase shorter-length screws.*

a room with a view

PLEXIGLAS ALBUM

I remember seeing a really cool restaurant menu made from Plexiglas. That's why I found myself in a hardware store asking, "Excuse me, sir, do you cut Plexiglas sheets?" Sure enough, 10 minutes later I had a stack of Plexiglas and the beginnings of a new album that shows off my scrapbooking room.

product

Without a doubt, I am first and foremost inspired by product, and I simply love having them displayed to look at on my shelves. Most times I will create an entire album, or concept an idea before ever knowing what will fill its pages. I feel the most creative freedom when allowing myself to scrapbook this way. I get great satisfaction from finding a new product and creating an entire project around it.

circle letters

quare letters

the best things come in small packages

inspiration

Not only is my scrapbooking space filled with colorful product, but it is also filled with some of my favorite jars, tins and vintage items that I have collected over the years. It is these small, but aesthetically valuable objects that I enjoy most when looking about in my space. They are my visual inspirations and undoubtedly contribute to many of my project designs. I often arrange and switch out products so that I have a constant source of new inspiration.

envision, inspire, create...simplicity

ADHESIVE

- **glue stick**
- **photo tabs**

MATERIALS

packing tape (3M) • hand drill (Fiskars) • ribbon (Offray, Textured Trios, May Arts) • Arial font

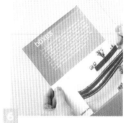

STEP SIX

Place (do not adhere) printed cardstock behind the Plexiglas.

STEP SEVEN

Drill a hole through the upper left corner of the Plexiglas and cardstock. *Note: Use a clamp to secure the Plexiglas as you drill, or have someone hold it for you.*

STEP EIGHT

Secure cardstock to the back of the Plexiglas with ribbon. Tie in front. Adhere ribbon to Plexiglas with photo tabs. Place completed pages on a large binder ring.

Helpful Tip

I used 4" packing tape on this project. If you don't have that size, use two strips of 2" packing tape, placed side by side.

SUPPLIES

- one roll, clear 4" packing tape
- 16" x 24" piece of Plexiglas cut into six 6" x 8" pieces
- six photocopied photographs
- six 6" x 8" pieces of white cardstock
- six 24" lengths of assorted ribbon
- 2" binder ring

TOOLS

- hand drill and large drill bit
- paper trimmer
- water bucket and paper towels
- bone folder

plexiglas album step-by-step

STEP ONE

To transfer image, cut and apply clear packing tape over a photocopied image. *Note: Image MUST be photocopied. Pictures printed from a laser or ink-jet printer will not transfer.* Use a bone folder or straight edge ruler to ensure that there are no bubbles in your tape.

STEP TWO

Soak paper with tape in a bucket of warm water for at least 10 min. While the paper is submerged in water, rub your fingers vigorously along the back of tape to remove the paper. *Note: Remove all paper or the tape will not stick.* Repeat for each photo.

STEP THREE

Gently shake off excess water from tape and set on a paper towel, sticky side up. Let dry. *Note: Once tape is dry, it will regain its stickiness.*

STEP FOUR

Firmly press tape to Plexiglas page. *Note: Darker portions of image will tend to be less sticky, due to the amount of toner that was transferred.* Use glue stick to apply adhesive to the less-sticky portions of your tape.

STEP FIVE

Print title and journaling on the top half of cardstock (see "Printing Reverse Text" on p. 17).

signs of home

Going back to my childhood home always triggers a whirlwind of emotions. Everything appears smaller than I remember, and I'm immediately transported back in time to the pizza joint where I wiped mozzarella off my chin or the 7-Eleven where I guzzled a lot of Big Gulps. But the first thing I always look for are the signs—specifically the green and white signs along the New Jersey Parkway—that indicate I'm almost home. This is the kind of scrapbook that unleashes a flood of memories.

DON'S PIZZA KING

DON'S PIZZA KING IS AN ICON. A SMALL PIZZA PARLOR THAT OFFERED VIDEO GAMES, A JUKEBOX AND SHELTER FROM THE COLD. MANY A SODA AND SLICES WERE HAD HANGING OUT WITH FRIENDS...ON ST. PATRICK'S DAY THEY WOULD SERVE GREEN PIZZA.

COMO LAKE

ON SUNDAYS AFTER CHURCH, WITH A BAG OF STALE BREAD IN HAND, MOM AND I WOULD HEAD TO COMO LAKE TO FEED THE DUCKS AND GEESE.

MATERIALS

patterned paper (Chatterbox) • metal frame (Making Memories)

STEP SIX
Embellish the cover with metal frame and title.

STEP SEVEN
Sandwich the pages between the front and back covers, and have the album professionally wire-bound at a local office supply or copy store. *Note: Call ahead to make sure they can bind books.*

Helpful Tip

To type journaling for each page, change page orientation to landscape. Create a 5" square text box and place it on the far left of the page. Type your text, so that it's right justified. And be sure to leave a space for the cardstock strip between the page title and the journaling.

SUPPLIES

- two 7" x 12" pieces of patterned paper
- two 5" x 10" pieces of chipboard
- two 4¾" x 9¾" pieces of cardstock
- 8½" x 11" pieces of cardstock in two coordinated shades

- small metal frame

TOOLS
- paper trimmer

spiral-bound album step-by-step

STEP ONE
To create the front and back covers, use patterned paper to cover chipboard (see "Wrapping Chipboard Covers" on p. 15).

STEP TWO
Adhere cardstock to unfinished sides of covers.

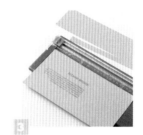

STEP THREE
Print text on 8½" x 11" cardstock, then trim each page to 5" x 10" (see "Helpful Tip" on p. 56).

STEP FOUR
Cut 10" x ⅛" strips of cardstock and adhere between the title and journaling on each page.

STEP FIVE
Trim photos to 4" squares. Mat with cardstock, leaving ¼" border. Adhere to page. *Note: Keep the page design the same throughout the album. Alternate two coordinating shades of cardstock for a simple, balanced look.*

before I was
a mom

a collection of
photos and stories
from my childhood

before i was a mom

Although it's hard for my kids to believe, I had a life before I became a mom. Just to prove the point (and to revel in a little nostalgia), I customized a pre-made album by trimming its full-sized page in half and added plenty of photos and journaling about those days before sticky high-chairs, boo-boos, and exhaustion.

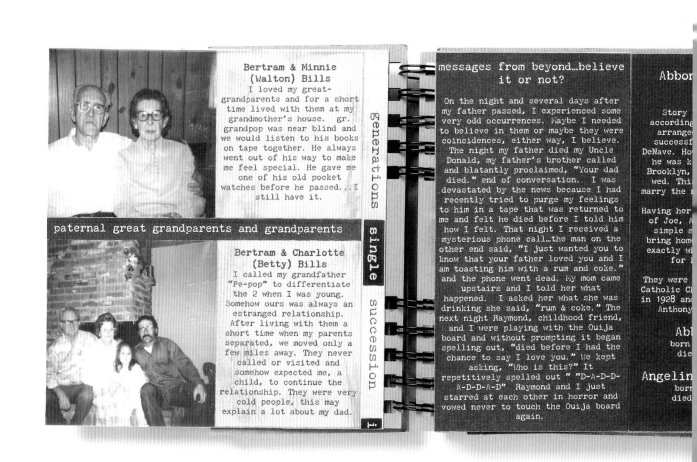

Bertram & Minnie (Walton) Bills

I loved my great-grandparents and for a short time lived with them at my grandmother's house. gr. grandpop was near blind and we would listen to his books on tape together. He always went out of his way to make me feel special. He gave me one of his old pocket watches before he passed...I still have it.

paternal great grandparents and grandparents

Bertram & Charlotte (Betty) Bills

I called my grandfather "Pe-pop" to differentiate the 2 when I was young. Somehow ours was always an estranged relationship. After living with them a short time when my parents separated, we moved only a few miles away. They never called or visited and somehow expected me, a child, to continue the relationship. They were very cold people, this may explain a lot about my dad.

generations single succession

messages from beyond...believe it or not?

On the night and several days after my father passed, I experienced some very odd occurrences. Maybe I needed to believe in them or maybe they were coincidences, either way, I believe.

The night my father died my Uncle Donald, my father's brother called and blatantly proclaimed, "Your dad died." end of conversation. I was devastated by the news because I had recently tried to purge my feelings to him in a tape that was returned to me and felt he died before I told him how I felt. That night I received a mysterious phone call...the man on the other end said, "I just wanted you to know that your father loved you and I am toasting him with a rum and coke." and the phone went dead. My mom came upstairs and I told her what happened. I asked her what she was drinking she said, "rum & coke." The next night Raymond, childhood friend, and I were playing with the Ouija board and without prompting it began spelling out, "died before I had the chance to say I love you." We kept asking, "Who is this?" It repetitively spelled out " D-A-D-D-A-D-D-A-D" Raymond and I just starred at each other in horror and vowed never to touch the Ouija board again.

Abbon

Story according arrange successf DeNave. Ho he was k Brooklyn, wed. This marry the

Having her of Joe, A simple m bring home exactly w for

They were Catholic Cl in 1928 a Anthony

Ab
born
die

Angelin
born
died

ADHESIVE

- **Xyron machine**
- **photo tabs**

MATERIALS

gated album (7gypsies) • patterned paper, stickers (Pebbles Inc.) • pre-printed transparencies (Creative Imaginations, K&Company.) • stamp pad (Ranger Industries) • brads (Making Memories) • bookplates (*twopeasinabucket.com*, Li'l Davis Designs) • ribbon (Offray) • American Typewriter font

STEP SIX

Print journaling on cardstock. Ink edges, and adhere to pages.

STEP SEVEN

Adhere patterned paper to section pages, e.g., "Legacy," "Childhood," and "School Days." Attach transparencies over patterned paper, using bookplates and brads.

STEP EIGHT

Embellish pages using photos and stickers.

STEP NINE

Tie off album by threading ribbon between the back cover and last page of the album. Tie in front.

Helpful Tips

Choose a color scheme and embellishments that won't compete with your photos, and keep them the same throughout the album. To maintain a consistent design, try adding a sticker strip down the sides of each full page.

Working with a pre-made album requires a little more planning. Create a framework for the theme and subjects you wish to include and decide how many pages you need to allot for each. For example, my framework includes:

- Family legacy—family photos and stories
- Childhood journey—favorite photos and stories of my childhood from my mother's perspective
- School days—school photos and sentiments, plus a series of prom photos and fashions (eek)
- College years—a collection of photos and stories describing my life post-high school, including the story of how I met my husband
- Memorabilia—report cards, miscellaneous photos, etc.

gated album step-by-step

STEP ONE

Place sticker strips on left and right sides of gated cover. Print title on cardstock, cut to 5¾" x 7½". *Note: Check the spacing and make sure the gatefold opening will not open through any words.*

STEP TWO

Ink cardstock edges and apply gray chalk (see "Chalking" on p. 16).

STEP THREE

Adhere title page to left-side cover; right half of title page will hang over.

STEP FOUR

Trim off right half of title page and adhere to right-side cover.

STEP FIVE

To create album pages, cut random pages in half, using a paper trimmer.

my travels

Moved by the art and architecture I had seen from my travels in Europe, I wanted to find the perfect canvas from which to create a small travel album. While browsing the art aisles of my local craft store, I found packs of canvas mat boards. I embellished each one with photos and journaling from each city I visited, and tied them all together with ribbon and a handle to remind me of a little suitcase.

TOOLS
- paper trimmer
- hand drill and large drill bit
- foam brushes
- pencil and eraser
- scissors

ADHESIVE
- Xyron machine
- dots

MATERIALS

paint, metal-rimmed tags, rub-on letters (Making Memories) • ribbon (Offray) • rub-on dates (Autumn Leaves) • rubber stamps (Limited Edition Rubberstamps, Green Pepper Press) • stamp pad (Tsukineko) • hand drill (Fiskars)

STEP SEVEN

Drill two holes in mat boards for binding and handle, approx. 2" from the sides, and ⅜" from the spine (see "Craft hand drill" on p. 13).

STEP EIGHT

Place photos in "paint frames."

STEP NINE

To embellish, place rub-on dates on metal-rimmed tags. Thread jump rings through holes of bulldog clips and place clips over photos on the front pages.

STEP TEN

Thread ribbons through the holes of all six mat boards. Thread through holes of handle and tie in bows. *Note: Make knot large enough so ribbon does not slip through. Use ribbon that is at least ¾" wide to secure the weight of the canvas mat boards.*

canvas mat board album step-by-step

STEP ONE
Brush two colors of acrylic paint across the front of each canvas mat board. Let dry.

STEP TWO
Use stamps or rub-ons to create the album title on one mat board. Set aside.

STEP THREE
On remaining mat boards, use stamps and rub-ons to add titles. *Note: Leave room for photos.* Adhere photos with dots.

STEP FOUR
For the back of each page, handwrite or print journaling on cardstock. *Note: I set my margins in Microsoft Word, printed my text on 8½" x 11", and trimmed.*

STEP FIVE
Lightly paint edges of cardstock. Create a "paint frame" by gently sweeping edges of brush along pencil marks. Let dry.

STEP SIX
Add photos and adhere cardstock pages to back of canvas boards.

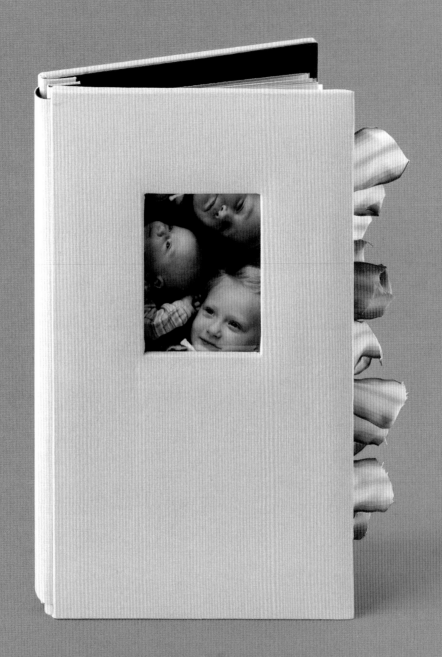

what do you do all day?

There's more to life than milestones—there's the everyday activities that form the bulk of existence. So I filled this 6" x 12" post-bound album with random snapshots of my day: hanging out in the backyard with the kids, going to the movies, picking strawberries. For added flair, I included large tags between each page protector to allow extra space for more photos—and more opportunities to celebrate the little things.

ADHESIVE

- **double-sided adhesive tape**

MATERIALS

post-bound album (Westrim) • tags (DMD, Inc.) • labeler (Dymo) • ribbon (Offray) • stamp pad (Ranger Industries) • Arial font

Helpful Tip

For a minimum investment, you can purchase multi-lens cameras that offer new photo options. The Lomographic Pop 9 takes nine identical pictures of your subject simultaneously while the Lomographic Super-sampler takes four shots in quick sequence on a single photo. For more information on lomographic photography, see *shop.lomography.com*.

post-bound album step-by-step

STEP ONE
Print or write text on 4" x 6" piece of cardstock. Adhere to top or bottom of 6" x 12" page.

STEP TWO
Create 6" word strip, using labeler, and adhere across the width of the page where the two cardstock pieces meet.

STEP THREE
Trim three portrait-oriented photos to a size slightly smaller than 6" x 2". Adhere to page.

STEP FOUR
Print or write text on one side of tag.

STEP FIVE
Ink edges (see "Inking" on p. 16), and tie ribbon through tag hole.

STEP SIX
Trim additional photos and adhere to tag. *Note: You can use one, two or three small, individual photos on the tag, or use a multi-lens camera such as the Lomographic Pop 9 or Lomographic Supersampler (see "Helpful Tip" on p. 68).*

STEP SEVEN
Score tags ¾" from bottom, and adhere to the seam of page protectors using double-sided tape. *Note: Vary the placement of your tags.*

circle of friends

There are two things a woman should never take for granted: the fit of a comfy pair of jeans and the company of good friends. With this in mind, I created this scrapbook to celebrate the friendships I have made with some spectacular women. The album was passed among nine of my friends, each of whom completed her own two-page spread before passing it along. It's an amazing keepsake, and a story of the journeys we have taken along the road of friendship.

MATERIALS

patterned paper (7gypsies, SEI, Chatterbox) • rub-ons, foam stamps, acrylic paint, eyelets, leather flowers, brads, mailbox letters, metal-rimmed tag (Making Memories) • hand drill (Fiskars) • woven label (me & my BIG ideas) • filmstrip (Creative Imaginations) •stamp pad (Ranger Industries) • ribbon (Offray) • Attic Antique and Caslon Regular fonts

STEP SIX

Thread each piece of leather cording through covers and pages. Tie to bind. Send album to first participant!

STEP SEVEN

To create pages, untie binding and remove chipboard pages. Adhere papers, photos, and embellishments directly to chipboard and punch holes for binding. Rethread page to reassemble.

Helpful Tip

The number of chipboard pages you make will vary depending on the number of participants in the album. Just be sure to include enough pages for everyone to create her entries.

SHE WAS JUST THIS NAME,

blue jean chipboard album step-by-step

STEP ONE
Cover cardboard with 10" x 9" sheets of patterned paper (see "Wrapping Chipboard Covers" on p. 15).

STEP TWO
Trim jeans around back pocket to measure 8¼" x 7¼". Trim another 8¼" x 7¼" section from jean's leg. Adhere denim to uncovered side of cardboard, using adhesive sheet. Press firmly, then trim off any excess denim hanging over edges.

STEP THREE
Use rub-on letters for "circle of" and stamp "friends" with acrylic paint.

STEP FOUR
Drill two holes through covers, about 1½" from top and bottom, and ½" from spine. Drill holes through chipboard pages at same spots (see "Craft hand drill" on p. 13).

STEP FIVE
Set eyelets in covers. *Note: Eyelets will not completely reach through the cardboard because of its thickness, so use a hammer and setter to force eyelet ends into the sides of cardboard (see "Setting Eyelets" on p. 16).*

a true friend

With almost 20 years of friendship between us, my friend Karen and I have plenty of stories to tell, and lots of secrets to keep. I made this little scrapbook, using ordinary office supply coin envelopes as pages, to tell our own story—from the laughter to the tears to the experiences that have shaped our lives. Hidden inside each envelope are special sentiments and secrets.

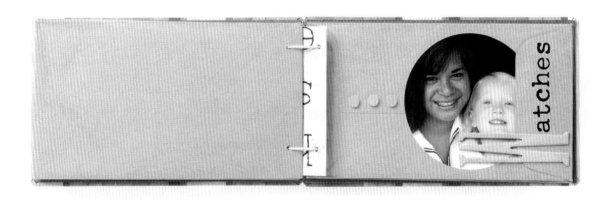

A true friend...
shares
the most important moments of their life with you.

Even on her wedding day Karen saw to it to throw the bouquet directly into my hands and then the garter into Bill's. At the most spectacular moment in her life, she made sure I was the one she passed the proverbial wedding torch too.

STEP SEVEN

Drill two holes approx. 3/4" from the top and bottom and 3/8" from the end. Drill through the entire spine including covers, folds, and envelopes (see "Craft hand drill" on p. 13).

STEP EIGHT

Set eyelets in front and back covers. *Note: Eyelet end may not reach all the way through chipboard, so place the setter in the underside hole and hit with a hammer to secure the eyelet.*

STEP NINE

Thread elastic up from the back cover to the front cover through the metal-rimmed tag and down through the other side.

STEP TEN

Use circle punch to cut out photos. Adhere to pages. Embellish album using rub-ons and stencil letters. *Note: Paint one stencil letter for each envelope. Use a hand punch to punch small circles from the unused portion of the stencil and place next to photo.*

STEP ELEVEN

Print journaling (see "Printing Journaling" on p. 17) on cardstock and place in envelopes.

coin envelope album step-by-step

STEP ONE

Wrap 5¾" x 8¼" pieces of patterned paper over chipboard (see "Wrapping Chipboard Covers" p. 15).

STEP TWO

To create the accordion spine, adhere two 3¼" x 12" strips back to back so that the patterned sides face out. Repeat with two more strips.

STEP THREE

Accordion-fold each strip every ¾", and adhere the two strips together. Trim your accordion so that you have 12 valleys. *Note: The envelopes will sit in each valley.*

STEP FOUR

Adhere front and back covers to the ends of the accordion, making sure everything is centered.

STEP FIVE

Adhere 6" x 3½" cardstock pieces to the undersides of each cover to hide the unfinished edges.

STEP SIX

Ink 10 coin envelopes (see "Inking" on p. 16). Place (do *not* adhere) and center one coin envelope in each valley of the accordion.

family

This album is dear to my heart. Layered inside each envelope is a personal story to my children reflecting on the joys of motherhood and our family. Albums like this make great keepsakes, and in some ways they're therapeutic, too. It's a chance to tell my kids those things I'd always wanted to say—if only they'd sit still long enough to listen.

MATERIALS

Coluzzle nested envelope template, swivel knife, mat (Provo Craft) • patterned paper (Paper House Productions, Chatterbox) • corrugated cardstock (Scrapbooks 'N More) • button snaps (Cloud 9 Design) • eyelets, brads (Making Memories) • family metal word (Pressed Petals) • transparency (K&Company) • ribbon (Paper House Productions, May Arts) • P22 Cezanne Regular and Avant Garde fonts

STEP SEVEN

In the second valley, adhere envelope to the right side. *Note: Be sure the envelope is centered top-to-bottom within the valley.* Secure with three eyelets. Repeat above step for remaining three envelopes, adhering envelopes in the third, fourth and fifth valleys.

STEP EIGHT

Adhere ribbon across inside back cover.

STEP NINE

In the first valley in the back, adhere back cover to the right side. In the first valley in the front, adhere front cover to the left side.

STEP TEN

Adhere cardstock pieces to inside front and back covers.

STEP ELEVEN

Embellish envelopes with journaling and photos. Attach tag, transparency, and flower to smaller flaps with brads (see photo on p. 81).

STEP TWELVE

Use sheer ribbon to close envelopes with button snap closures.

SUPPLIES

- two 5½" x 7¼" pieces of chipboard
- two 7½" x 9¼" pieces of patterned paper
- two 5¾" x 12" pieces of patterned paper
- four 12" x 12" pieces of corrugated paper
- two 5¼" x 7" pieces of cardstock
- eight button snaps
- 30" length of ribbon
- four 6" lengths of sheer ribbon
- 12 eyelets and silk flower

TOOLS

- paper trimmer
- 8¾" x 11" envelope template
- swivel knife and cutting mat
- eyelet-setting tools
- bone folder

envelope accordion album step-by-step

STEP ONE
Cover chipboard with 7½" x 9¼" patterned paper (see "Wrapping Chipboard Covers" on p. 15).

STEP TWO
To create accordion spine, adhere two 5¾" x 12" patterned paper strips back to back, so that the patterned sides face out.

STEP THREE
Accordion-fold strip lengthwise every 1", using bone folder.

STEP FOUR
Cut four envelopes from corrugated paper. *Note: You can use regular cardstock.* Score and fold envelope flaps.

STEP FIVE
Open envelope and lay flat. Use anywhere hole punch and hammer to punch hole through larger envelope flaps (centered lengthwise). Attach button snaps through holes. Repeat for remaining three envelopes. *Note: Instead of button snaps, set an eyelet through the center of a small circle of cardstock.*

STEP SIX
Lay out accordion-folded strip so that the two ends point up.

favorite family photos 2004

Sometimes after I finish an album, I'm so darn proud of how it turned out that I want to make one for everyone I know. But I just don't have that kind of time—or stamina. Thank goodness someone at Shutterfly, an online photo service, was smart enough to come up with this stylish, cost-effective solution. Upload some photos, type in some journaling, and everyone can get a copy. Plus, your sanity remains intact.

ADHESIVE

- none

MATERIALS

shutterfly.com • ribbon (Making Memories, Offray)

Helpful Tips

If you've been leery of digital scrapbooking, then fear no more! Shutterfly walks you through every step. I couldn't believe how easy it was. And the album looks like a professionally published book.

You can have up to six photos per page with the larger, hardcover books, or four photos per page with the smaller, softcover books. And the albums make perfect baby or wedding gifts.

Don't forget to incorporate a few journaling captions into your Shutterfly design. Some heartfelt sentences will make the book more meaningful.

shutterfly photo album step-by-step

STEP ONE

Visit *shutterfly.com* and establish an account by clicking "Sign up." *Note: There is no charge to open an account.*

STEP TWO

Click "Shutterfly Store."

STEP THREE

Click "Photo Books" on left side of screen.

STEP FOUR

Click "Get started." Select black suede cover. Click "Next." Select simple style. Click "Next." *Note: Choose from a variety of album covers, colors, styles, and layouts. The hardcover books measure 8¾" x 11¼" and the soft cover books measure 5½" x 7½".*

STEP FIVE

To complete the album, follow the simple, step-by-step prompts and instructions. *Note: It takes about a week to receive the album in the mail.*

STEP SIX

Wrap ribbon around front cover and tie (see photo on p. 82).

FLIP-FLOP ACCORDION ALBUM

This past fall I lugged kids, snacks, and camera to my daughter's soccer games, and by the end of the season I'd accumulated dozens of photos. The season was even more special because Daddy was McKenna's first coach. To highlight the two-fold importance of this experience, I created a flip-flop accordion album. If you think you have flipped all the way through the album, keep flipping—there's a whole new story on the other side.

ADHESIVE
- **Xyron machine**
- **photo tabs**

MATERIALS

patterned paper (Karen Foster Design) • bookplate, transparency, stickers (Creative Imaginations) • eyelet (Scrap Arts) • soccer ball eyelet (*scrapbookdetails.com*) • ribbon (Textured Trios) • metal-rimmed tag, brads (Making Memories) • stamp pad (Ranger Industries) • rub-on date (Autumn Leaves) • Misproject font

Print journaling in reverse text on two pieces of 5¾" x 5¾" white cardstock (see "Printing Reverse Text" on p. 17). Adhere journaling pages to chipboard covers, covering the unfinished edges.

Ink edges of remaining 5¾" x 5¾" pieces of white cardstock. Adhere each piece to front and backs of all 10 inside panels.

Use photo tabs to adhere transparency sheets to four of the panels. *Note: Put tabs in the center of the transparencies so the photos will hide the adhesive.*

Place photos throughout the album. Use clear stickers, rub-on date, ribbon, and metal-rimmed tag to finish album.

step-by-step

Wrap chipboard with patterned paper (see "Wrapping Chipboard Covers" on p. 15).

Place bookplate on cover. Use paper piercer and push pad to create holes for brads. Secure bookplate with brads. Set soccer ball eyelet.

Fold each 6" x 12" strip of cardstock in half lengthwise, and reopen to a "mountain" shape.

Adhere insides of two mountains to create a "Z" shape.

Attach inside of a third mountain to inside of second mountain. Repeat with fourth, fifth, and sixth pieces.

Adhere front cover, making sure it opens to the left. Turn the album over and adhere back cover (it should also open to the left).

a lifetime of memories

ROLODEX ALBUM

I wanted to scrapbook umpteen boxes of not-so-great holiday photos without spending 10 years doing it. The Rolodex album is my solution. Not only am I scrapbooking dozens of sub-par photos that I just can't throw away, I'm also reducing the guilt associated with my failure to scrapbook all those events. So go through your boxes of photos and pull out one photo from each event you planned on scrapbooking— you'll be surprised how liberating it can be.

2003 - On Your 3rd birthday, You wanted to make your own Happy Birthday cake. We went to the store & You picked out your mix & icing all by Yourself. You even bought m&m's to cover your cake in.

MATERIALS

patterned paper (Chatterbox, Karen Foster Design, me & my BIG ideas, 7gypsies) • definition sticker, metal-rimmed tags (Making Memories) • rub-on numbers (KI Memories, Autumn Leaves, Creative Imaginations, Scrapworks) • charms (K&Company) • ribbon (Making Memories, May Arts, Offray) • marker (Sakura)

STEP FIVE
To create event dividers, punch holes in bottom of alphabet stencil. Embellish with ribbon and charms or tags. Place paper covered cards behind stencil dividers.

STEP SIX
To create other dividers, adhere a 3" x 4" piece of cardstock to one side of Rolodex divider. Trim excess cardstock around divider and punch holes. Repeat with second piece of card-stock on other side of divider. Label with marker.

STEP SEVEN
File photo cards under appropriate theme, e.g., birthdays, Christmas, and school.

2002- by your 2nd birthday you were old enough to pick out your own outfit. Mr. Balloony man had left you a big bunch of balloons on the deck and you were running around the yard with them.

SUPPLIES

- 2¼" x 4" rotary card file (Rolodex)
- black marker
- rub-on numbers
- alphabet stencils
- assorted patterned papers
- 6" lengths of assorted ribbon
- assorted themed charms and tags
- 3" x 4" pieces of cardstock

TOOLS

- sanding block
- Rolodex punch
- scissors
- paper trimmer

rolodex album step-by-step

STEP ONE

Trim each photo to 2¼" x 4" and adhere to a card. Trim overhanging edges with scissors. *Note: For a weathered look, use a sanding block to file edges.*

STEP TWO

Punch holes in photos, using the holes in the card as a guide.

STEP THREE

Add journaling to the back of the card and embellish photos with rub-ons.

STEP FOUR

Using patterned paper instead of photos, repeat Steps 1 and 2 to cover several cards.

through the

YEARS

donna downey
1971-2005

through the years

4" X 6" PHOTO ALBUM

My family's favorite place for Sunday breakfast is Bob Evans Restaurant. While we wait to be seated, I like to slip away to the gift shop and read the *In the Year You Were Born* cards. They describe what the world was like in a given year—the popular tunes, TV shows, and events, etc., that defined the times. This album is inspired by those cards, and is a miniaturized chronicle of facts, trivia, and pop culture documenting each year of my life.

1971

Donna Christine Bills
is born September 17th at 5:34 PM
in Point Pleasant New Jersey
weighing 7lbs measuring 20 in.

Best Picture:
Patton

Song of the Year:
"Bridge Over Troubled Water," Paul Simon, songwriter

INTEL INTRODUCES THE MICRO-PROCESSOR.

PRESIDENT, RICHARD M. NIXON
VICE PRESIDENT, SPIRO T. AGNEW

Bread: $0.25/loaf
Milk: $1.32/gal
Eggs: $1.18/doz
New Car: $3,742
Gas: $0.36/gal

House: $28,300
Stamp: $0.08/ea
Income: $11,583/yr
Min.Wage: $1.60/hr

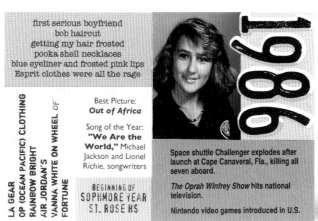

first serious boyfriend
bob haircut
getting my hair frosted
pooka shell necklaces
blue eyeliner and frosted pink lips
Esprit clothes were all the rage

1986

LA GEAR
OP (OCEAN PACIFIC) CLOTHING
RAINBOW BRIGHT
AIR JORDAN'S
VANNA WHITE ON WHEEL OF FORTUNE

Best Picture:
Out of Africa

Song of the Year:
"We Are the World," Michael Jackson and Lionel Richie, songwriters

BEGINNING OF
SOPHMORE YEAR
ST. ROSE HS

Space shuttle Challenger explodes after launch at Cape Canaveral, Fla., killing all seven aboard.

The Oprah Winfrey Show hits national television.

Nintendo video games introduced in U.S.

MATERIALS

4" x 6" photo album (Target) • stickers (Sticker Studio) • leather flowers (Making Memories) • brads (Bazzill Basics Paper) • Gill Sans, Helvetica Narrow Bold, and American Typewriter fonts

Helpful Tip

Looking for info to include on your pages? Try these websites:

infoplease.com/yearbyyear.html

vh1.com

fun4birthdays.com/year/index.html

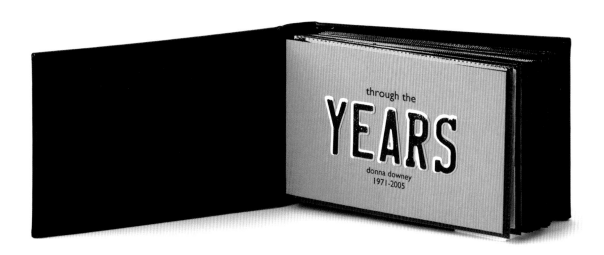

SUPPLIES

- 4" x 6" photo album
- several pieces of 4" x 6¼" cardstock
- five pieces of coordinating colored cardstock
- leather flowers
- mini brads
- number stickers

TOOLS

- paper trimmer
- paper piercer or push pin
- push pad

4" x 6" photo album step-by-step

STEP ONE
Sketch a color-blocking template on a 4" x 6¼" piece of cardstock. *Note: Each opposing page is a mirror image of the template, so you only have to create one template (see photo on p. 97).*

STEP TWO
Trace and cut cardstock blocks and one photo to size, using template.

STEP THREE
Print text on cardstock blocks. *Note: Measure block sizes and create text boxes accordingly (see "Printing Journaling" on p. 17). Save your text box document to use for remaining pages. To print on blocks, see "Printing Text on Tags" on p. 17.*

STEP FOUR
Arrange and adhere blocks on a clean piece of 4" x 6¼" cardstock. *Note: Don't adhere on your template.* Use number stickers for year.

STEP FIVE
Attach one leather flower with brad per two-page spread, using a paper piercer and push pad to create guide hole.

STEP SIX
Repeat for each page.

family recipes

BINDER BOARD ALBUM

It's really no secret that I do not know how to cook. Don't get me wrong, I do try, but thank goodness I married a man who is willing to eat just about anything I put down in front of him. So I started compiling an album of favorite family recipes. I asked family members to send me his or her favorite recipe along with a story or anecdote as to why it's a favorite; how could I go wrong, I figured, with a resource like this?

STEP FIVE

Print "Family Recipes" on 1¼" x 2¾" piece of card-stock. Place bookplate over title and attach to cover, using two eyelet snaps (see "Setting Eyelets" on p. 16).

STEP SIX

Add section titles to bottom of chipboard pages, using alphabet rub-on.

STEP SEVEN

Cut filler pages from card-stock to measure 5" wide and ¾" shorter than each of the lengths listed in Step 1. Ink edges. Print or write recipe and journaling.

STEP EIGHT

For opposing page, add pieces of inked patterned paper and photo. Punch holes and insert filler pages between coordinating section pages.

STEP NINE

Sand edges of section pages (see "Sanding" on p. 15).

Helpful Tip

Avoid using a decoupage adhesive such as Mod Podge for this album. The liquid adhesive may cause the chipboard pages to warp.

binder board album step-by-step

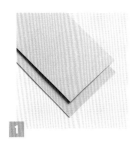

STEP ONE

Create cascading section pages from chipboard, each measuring 5¼" wide and ¾" shorter than the previous page. *Note: The page lengths should be 12", 11¼", 10½", 9¾", 9", 8¼", 7½", 6¾" and 6".*

STEP TWO

Cut two pieces, measuring the same as in Step 1, from each of the nine papers. Adhere one piece to the front and another to the back of each chipboard page. *Note: Do not wrap chipboard pages.*

STEP THREE

Before punching holes in chipboard pages, make a template on a piece of scrap paper to ensure that pages will fit loosely on binder spine. Punch holes in chipboard pages, using template as a guide. *Note: Save template to use with filler pages.*

STEP FOUR

Spray-paint plywood, binder spine, and bookplate. Let dry. Center and attach binder spine to board base with two screws.

confessions of a shopaholic

SHOPPING BAG ALBUM

I just can't pass up a sale. So while browsing the aisles of my local craft store, I found a bundle of these inexpensive brown craft bags and tossed them into my shopping cart. I figured they were versatile enough for almost anything, and I kept them with my stash of other impulse purchases. Several weeks later I ran across them again, and I realized…it's a scrapbook!

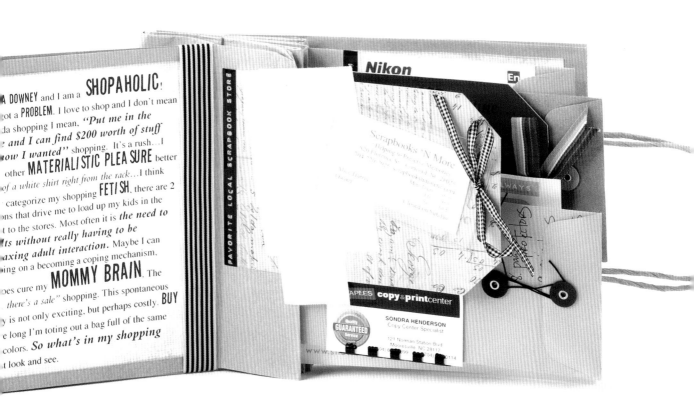

MATERIALS

string envelopes (Waste Not Paper) • large tag cards (K&Company) • metal trim (Making Memories) • ribbon (Textured Trios, Offray) • labeler (Dymo)• Two Peas Tasklist, Times, and Bembo Italic fonts • stamp pad (Ranger Industries) • hand drill (Fiskars)

STEP SEVEN

To create the inner pages, adhere various envelopes, large tags, or cardstock pieces within the inner flaps.

STEP EIGHT

Print or write journaling on both 8" x 7½" pieces of cardstock. Ink edges and adhere to front and back inside covers. Place metal trim on left side of cardstock.

STEP NINE

Embellish pages using ribbon, photos, stickers, and charms. *Note: Don't forget to open the bag handles and insert memorabilia, newspaper ads, or more journaling.*

STEP TEN

To create the cover, use reverse text printing (see "Printing Reverse Text" on p. 17). Wrap ribbon around front cover. Tie in bow.

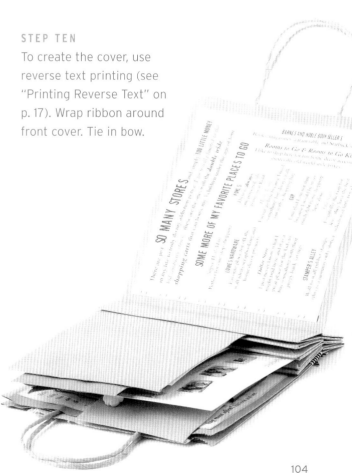

shopping bag album step-by-step

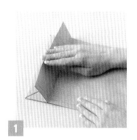

STEP ONE

Lay bag on flat surface with bottom flap showing. Fold bottom flap down towards the bottom of the bag so it creates a "Y" shape at the bottom. Repeat with another bag.

STEP TWO

Cut off bags 2" above the bottom flap. Discard tops.

STEP THREE

Layer the cut bottom portions, one on top of the other, so that you have four fanned flaps. Adhere cut sides together.

STEP FOUR

Lay an uncut bag on flat surface so that the bottom of the bag is not showing. Adhere bag bottom to the 2" portion of the cut bags.

STEP FIVE

Turn the entire album over and adhere another uncut bag to the back along the 2" portion of the cut bags.

STEP SIX

Using your prong fasteners as guides, mark where the four holes will be drilled for binding. Drill or punch holes through all four bags and bind with fasteners.

love

Everyone loves a little box. People like to pick them up and cradle them for a second or two before opening the lid. Heck, these things beg to be handled. This one has a surprise, though—an accordion fold commemorating the bond between my husband and me. But really it could be about anything, so think outside the box (or should I say inside the box?).

MATERIALS

patterned paper, stickers (American Crafts) • metal-rimmed tags, quote plaque, bookplate (Making Memories) • rub-ons (Creative Imaginations, Making Memories) • ribbon charms (Junkitz) • ribbon (Offray)

STEP FIVE

Place sticker on box lid.

SUPPLIES

- two 2½" x 12" pieces of cardstock
- 2¼" pâpier-maché box
- nine 2" squares of patterned paper
- rub-on letters and words
- two 8" lengths of ribbon
- two circle tags
- coordinated stickers
- quote plaque
- bookplate
- ribbon and ribbon charms

TOOLS

- paper trimmer with scoring blade

mini-box accordion step-by-step

STEP ONE
Accordion-fold each strip of cardstock every 2¼". Trim off any partial accordion pages.

STEP TWO
Adhere accordion strips together by placing the last page of the first accordion strip on top of the first page of the second accordion strip. *Note: To create a longer album, simply add more accordion strips.*

STEP THREE
Adhere patterned squares to each page. Place photos, rub-on letters and words, and remaining embellishments on pages.

STEP FOUR
Adhere back of first page to inside of box lid. Adhere back of last page to inside of box base.

cole

5¼" FLOPPY DISK ALBUM

Bette McIntyre, one of my loyal scrapbook students, pulled me aside one night after class and whipped a 5¼"
floppy disk from her bag. "I have six boxes of these darn things sitting in my closet," she said. "Do you think
you can do something with them?" The creative gears in my head immediately started to turn, and before
you could say "obsolete technology," I'd come up with this nifty little scrapbook. If you can't get your hands
on a box of 5¼" floppies, chipboard will do just as well.

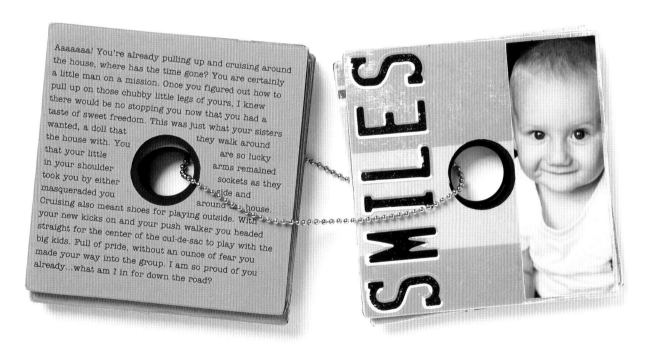

Aaaaaaa! You're already pulling up and cruising around
the house, where has the time gone? You are certainly
a little man on a mission. Once you figured out how to
pull up on those chubby little legs of yours, I knew
there would be no stopping you now that you had a
taste of sweet freedom. This was just what your sisters
wanted, a doll that they walk around the house with. You are so lucky that your little arms remained in your shoulder sockets as they took you by either side and masqueraded you around the house. Cruising also meant shoes for playing outside. With
your new kicks on and your push walker you headed
straight for the center of the cul-de-sac to play with the
big kids. Full of pride, without an ounce of fear you
made your way into the group. I am so proud of you
already...what am I in for down the road?

MATERIALS

Coluzzle nested circle template, swivel knife, mat (Provo Craft) • patterned paper (Basic Grey) • letter stickers (Sticker Studio) • beaded chain (Making Memories) • American Typewriter font

STEP FIVE

To round corners and add a weathered look, sand edges of cardstock and patterned paper.

STEP SIX

Bind all pages with beaded chain.

TOOLS

• paper trimmer

• large circle template

• swivel knife and mat

• sanding block

floppy disk album step-by-step

STEP ONE

Use circle template (see "Cutting template" on p. 13), or trace hole in floppy disk, to cut small circles in the center of each 5¼" x 5¼" square of patterned paper. *Note: The Coluzzle nested circle template has eight circles to choose from. Use the second circle from the center for this project.*

STEP TWO

Adhere to one side of each disk.

STEP THREE

Print or write journaling on cardstock and adhere to the other side of each disk. *Note: To print journaling, create a 4¾" x 4¾" text box (see "Printing Journaling" on p. 17). Insert 1½" circle auto shape in the center of the text box to mark the placement of the hole in the floppy disk.*

STEP FOUR

Trim seven photos to 1¾" x 5". Sand edges. Adhere each photo to seven of the disks. Add a title to each disk, using letter stickers.

111

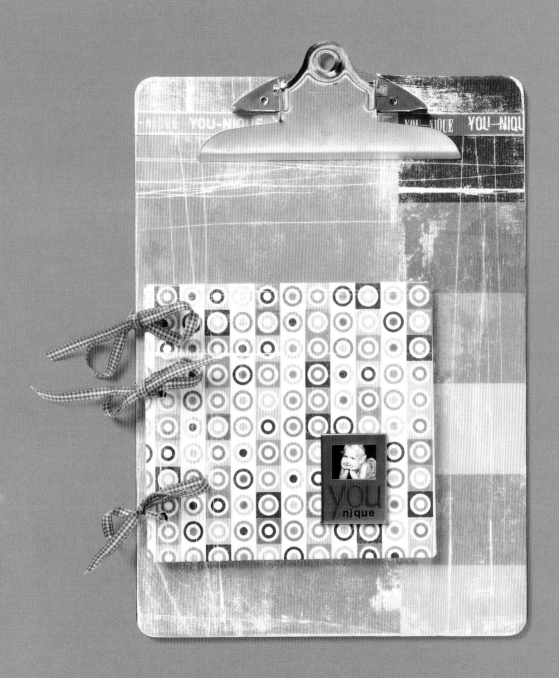

you-nique

My daughter Payton has this thing for shoes. She loves them all: sandals, sneakers, penny loafers, and boots. So I created this album from an inexpensive clipboard to showcase Payton's curious infatuation with shoes. By simply attaching a cover and filler pages to the altered clipboard, I have the perfect showcase for this amusing album.

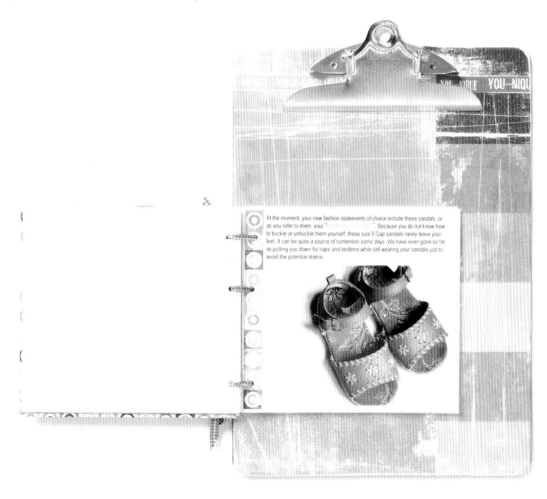

At the moment, your new fashion statements of choice include these sandals, or as you refer to them, your "_____". Because you do not know how to buckle or unbuckle them yourself, these size 9 Gap sandals rarely leave your feet. It can be quite a source of contention some days. We have even gone so far as putting you down for naps and bedtime while still wearing your sandals just to avoid the potential drama.

MATERIALS

patterned paper (Basic Grey) • frame (Scrapworks) • rub-ons (Scrapworks, Chartpak) • ribbon (Offray) • hand drill (Fiskars) • Arial Narrow font • decoupage adhesive (Plaid)

STEP FIVE

Create a computer-generated word strip on patterned paper, using reverse text printing (see "Printing Reverse Text" on p. 17). Lift clip and adhere strip across board along paper seams.

STEP SIX

Cut patterned paper to 8½" x 8", and cover chipboard (see "Wrapping Chipboard Covers" on p. 15). Adhere 6¼" x 5¾" piece of card-stock or patterned paper to inside front cover.

STEP SEVEN

Embellish metal frame with rub-ons, insert photo, and place on album cover.

STEP EIGHT

Adhere one ½" x 5¾" strip of patterned paper to left side of each 6½" x 6" piece of cardstock. Complete album pages using photos and journaling.

STEP NINE

Stack pages and cover; place on clipboard. Drill three holes approx. ¾" from left edge of clipboard. Drill through cover, pages, and clipboard. *Note: You'll need to secure the clipboard with a clamp or have someone hold it in place while you drill.*

STEP TEN

Thread ribbon through holes and tie to clipboard.

clipboard album step-by-step

STEP ONE

Cut patterned paper to 6½" x 12" and 3½" x 1" pieces. Brush coat of decoupage adhesive on left side of clipboard and underneath clip. Place larger piece of paper on clipboard, top edge flush with clip base. Use brayer to smooth out air bubbles or creases.

STEP TWO

Repeat Step 1 to cover top left-hand side of clipboard with smaller piece of paper. Trim around clip base, using craft knife. Let dry for 5 mins. Sand off excess edges.

STEP THREE

Cut patterned paper to 3½" x 12" and 3½" x 1" pieces. Brush coat of decoupage adhesive on right side of clipboard and underneath clip. Place larger piece of paper on clipboard, top edge flush with clip base. Use brayer to smooth out air bubbles or creases.

STEP FOUR

Repeat Step 3 to cover top right-hand side of clipboard with smaller piece of paper. Trim around clip base, using craft knife. Let dry for 5 mins. Sand off excess edges.

resources

Listed below are some of the companies whose products I used throughout the book. Although some of these companies only offer products wholesale, their websites make for great browsing and often will direct you to a retailer carrying their product. Be sure to enter *www.* before each Web address.

7gypsies
7gypsies.com

American Crafts
americancrafts.com

Autumn Leaves
autumnleaves.com

BasicGrey
basicgrey.com

Chartpak
chartpak.com

Chatterbox Inc.
chatterboxinc.com

Cloud 9 Design
cloud9design.biz

Creative Imaginations
cigift.com

DMD, Inc.
dmdind.com

Fiskars
fiskars.com

Junkitz
junkitz.com

K&Company
kandcompany.com

KI Memories
kimemories.com

Li'l Davis Designs
lildavisdesigns.com

Making Memories
makingmemories.com

May Arts
mayarts.com

Offray
offray.com

Paper Addict
paperaddict.com

Paper House Productions
paperhouseproductions.com

Pebbles Inc.
pebblesinmypocket.com

Plaid
plaidonline.com

Provo Craft
provocraft.com

Ranger Industries
rangerink.com

Scrapworks
scrapworks.com

Sticker Studio
stickerstudio.com

Two Peas in a Bucket
twopeasinabucket.com

Xyron
xyron.com

RETAIL STORES
Scrapbooks 'N More
scrapbooksnmorenc.com

Michaels
michaels.com

Target
target.com

CREATE

A self-proclaimed "paper product junkie," Donna Downey notes that scrapbooking is the ideal extension of her paper and photography addiction. As a contributing editor for *Simple Scrapbooks* magazine, she plays with the latest and greatest products, yet manages to keep the projects—and the process—simple and do-able.

Donna travels and teaches at scrapbook events across the country, inspiring students to think outside of the traditional scrapbook box, while still preserving their memories in a meaningful way.

A former elementary school teacher, Donna is a stay-at-home mom to her three children, McKenna, Payton and Cole. Originally from the Jersey shore, she now lives in North Carolina and teaches at her local scrapbook store. She tries to steal away as much quiet time as she can to scrapbook—which usually means she kicks it into gear at 1 a.m.

LAY

LIVE

CAROLYN VAUGHN PHOTOGRAPHY

119

yes, it's a scrapbook!

LOOK FOR MORE BOOKS BY DONNA DOWNEY

photo decor

Twenty-five amazing ways to display
memories and photos on the table or on the
wall. Step-by-step instructions and photos.

$14.95. 120 pages.

decorative journals

Twenty-five unique ideas for saving the
story of special moments and everyday life.
Step-by-step instructions and photos.

$14.95. 120 pages.

To order, call toll-free (866) 334-8149, visit your scrapbook store,

or shop online at **simplescrapbooksmag.com/shop**

redefine the term scrapbook

What do an old cigar box, a stack of used CDs, and a bunch of shopping bags have in common? To author **Donna Downey** they are all scrapbooks— yes, scrapbooks. As a contributing editor to *Simple Scrapbooks* magazine, Donna **redefines traditional scrapbooking** and inspires paper crafters to get out of their scrapbooking rut.

In *Creative Albums*, her first book in the *Yes, It's a Scrapbook!* series, Donna shares 25 "out of the box" ways to capture your most **meaningful memories**. And best of all, you can finish most albums in an afternoon or over a weekend.

Each project includes:

- Clear, **how-to** instructions
- **Step-by-step** photos
- **Color photos** of album covers and pages
- Complete **list of supplies** and tools needed

Give your new albums to friends and family, or show them off on the coffee table. Either way, you're sure to hear, "Wow! Is this a scrapbook?"

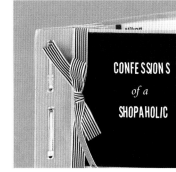

ISBN   1 929180 78 0
creative albums $14.95

6 15803 05050 5